Passion and Virtuosity

HENDRICK GOLTZIUS
AND THE ART OF ENGRAVING

WILLIAM BREAZEALE

VICTORIA SANCHO LOBIS

This catalogue is published
on the occasion of the exhibition

Passion and Virtuosity

HENDRICK GOLTZIUS
AND THE ART OF ENGRAVING

Crocker Art Museum, Sacramento
20 October 2013–26 January 2014

Robert and Karen Hoehn Family Galleries
University of San Diego
21 February–25 May 2014

William Breazeale
Victoria Sancho Lobis
Curators

Design Leah Roschke, StudioGrafik
Editor Julie Dunn
Publication Oversight Victoria Sancho Lobis

Copyright © 2013 University of San Diego
5998 Alcalá Park, San Diego, CA 92110

ISBN# 0-9760854-6-1

Printed in the United States of America by Neyenesch Printers

COVER
Hendrick Goltzius (1558–1617)
The Last Supper (The Passion), 1598 (detail)
Engraving, 20.1 x 13.4 cm
University of San Diego
Purchased with Funds from Robert and Karen Hoehn

CONTENTS

Jacob Matham (1571–1631)
Portrait of Hendrick Goltzius (after Hendrick Goltzius), 1617
Engraving, 43.3 x 28.8 cm
The Hearn Family Trust

DIRECTORS' FOREWORD

Though his name is less well known today, Hendrick Goltzius was as important to the art of engraving as Rembrandt van Rijn was to etching. Goltzius's virtuoso technique and engaging treatment of subjects combined to make him one of the most sought-after printmakers throughout the late sixteenth and early seventeenth centuries, and for centuries afterwards. Today, his work occupies a central place in the finest collections of European prints. It is a great pleasure, therefore, for the Crocker Art Museum and University Galleries at the University of San Diego to collaborate by bringing his two most important series of engravings—the *Birth and Early Life of Christ* (or the *Masterpieces*) and the *Passion*—together in an exhibition. This project examines the origin, context, and importance of these seldom seen works, together with some comparative works by Albrecht Dürer, Lucas van Leyden, and others, providing a fresh scholarly perspective on the legacy of Hendrick Goltzius and his work as an engraver.

In the course of preparing such an ambitious exhibition, we have enjoyed the cooperation of numerous lenders, both public and private. We wish to acknowledge our colleagues at the Los Angeles County Museum of Art: Claudine Dixon, Michael Govan, Britt Salvesen, and Naoko Takahatake; at the Achenbach Foundation for Graphic Arts at the Fine Arts Museums of San Francisco: Colin Bailey, Jim Ganz; at the Hammer Museum at UCLA: Cynthia Burlingham, Annie Philbin. Private lenders Robert Getscher and Harry Wilkinson of Cleveland and Norman Leitman of San Diego have made their collections available for study and exhibition as well as other lenders who wish to remain anonymous. Yana van Dyke, conservator at The Metropolitan Museum of Art, also provided professional support, for which we are grateful. In San Diego, Janet Ruggles and colleagues at Balboa Art Conservation Center have facilitated the preparation of objects for exhibition. We also wish to thank colleagues in the prints and drawings world who have extended their support for this project at critical points in its development: Nancy Bialler, Charles Hack, Lee Hendrix, Suzanne Folds McCullagh, Nadine Orenstein, Stephanie Schrader, Nancy Yocco.

This handsome catalogue would not be possible without the generous support of Robert and Karen Hoehn, admirers of Hendrick Goltzius's oeuvre and passionate supporters of research on old master prints. Both the Crocker Art Museum and the University Galleries are grateful to Bob and Karen for their inspired philanthropy.

At the Crocker Art Museum, we wish to especially acknowledge John Caswell who provided expert assistance with loan documentation and shipping arrangements. At the University Galleries, Andrea Feliciano helped with loan requests, framing, and insurance issues; Catherine Childs helped prepare exhibition checklists and installation plans. This project would not have been possible without the curatorial efforts of Victoria Sancho Lobis and William Breazeale, curators at the University of San Diego and the Crocker Art Museum, respectively. We seize this opportunity to underscore our appreciation for their collaborative approach to this important work and for all of their efforts that have made this exhibition not just possible but worthwhile for our audiences.

Derrick R. Cartwright
Director, University Galleries
University of San Diego

Lial A. Jones
Mort and Marcy Friedman Director
Crocker Art Museum

Introduction

WILLIAM BREAZEALE
VICTORIA SANCHO LOBIS

*B*orn into an extended family of artists and publishers, Hendrick Goltzius (1558–1617) became one of the most revered and celebrated artists of his generation, gaining recognition from princes, cardinals, and collectors not only at home in the northern Netherlands but throughout Europe. Most widely known during his lifetime through his engravings and chiaroscuro woodcuts, Goltzius also completed an impressive body of drawings and paintings, which helped cement his reputation as a leading figure in what many now call International Mannerism. A prominent figure in the city of Haarlem, where he worked from 1577 until his death in 1617, Goltzius remained dedicated to his identity as an individual. He established his own printing press in 1582, thereby securing his artistic and financial independence. After a long-anticipated trip to Italy in 1590–91, Goltzius returned to Haarlem to embark on the most prolific and perhaps most artistically successful decade of his life. It was during these final years of the sixteenth century that he created two series of engravings, the *Birth and Early Life of Christ* (also known as the *Life of the Virgin* or the *Masterpieces*) and the *Passion*, which continue, more than four centuries later, to provide some of the most compelling and finely wrought examples of the art of engraving.

Over the course of his career as a printmaker, Goltzius was responsible for the execution, design, or inspiration for over 750 prints.[1] His distinctive style of engraving—often characterized by a swelling and tapering line used to emphasize the illusion of volume—was adopted by a workshop of his students and followers. The deftness with which he wielded his pen and burin set new standards for the art of *teykenkonst*, the art of design, so enthusiastically championed by friend and biographer Karel van Mander (1548–1606). Goltzius's desire to create art as a credit to his name is reflected in several drawings representing his personal motto, *Eer boven Golt* (Honor above Gold). In a pen and ink version from 1609 included in this exhibition (fig. 1), we find a winged genius crowned with hero's laurels facing the sun and levitating over a pot of gold coins and other vessels of luxury. Mercury's symbol, the caduceus (also the symbol frequently adopted by artists and artists' guilds), connects the upper and lower halves of the composition. Goltzius places his monogram (HG) in the center of the pot of gold, but his name also appears in abbreviated form (Golt) in the letters of the motto itself. Goltzius's motto also appears in a posthumous portrait print published in 1618 (fig. 2) and in two later editions of 1620 and 1630; the motto falls below the artist's likeness as another type of portrait together with a representation of the phoenix, a bird that rises from the ashes, which appears above the artist's head.

Goltzius left behind several examples of metaphorical self-portraits, such as the motto drawings, but he also created a number of self-portraits that are descriptive of his physical likeness. In a small roundel drawing executed with black chalk and colored chalk with opaque white watercolor (fig. 3), the viewer encounters a description of the artist as a middle-aged man with a blond beard and receding

FIGURE 1
Hendrick Goltzius (1558–1617)
The Artist's Emblem, 1609
Pen and brown ink (actual size)
Crocker Art Museum, E. B. Crocker Collection

hairline. His status as an artist is left unspecified in favor of the bourgeois trappings of a wide ruff collar and black doublet. Only the keen stare from the figure's clear blue eyes suggests that visual acuity provides for the sitter's success. By the time of the drawing, the early years of the seventeenth century, Goltzius had entrusted the operation of his printing workshop to his son-in-law Jacob Matham (1571–1631), who oversaw the production of prints based on designs by Goltzius and by other artists. In his final years, Goltzius devoted his time to drawings and paintings and to a rarely seen type of art called 'pen work,' which mimics the appearance of engraved lines but, in fact, is produced as large-scale drawings in pen and ink on canvas supports. After several bouts of ill health and a lifetime of struggle with physical limitations, Goltzius died on New Year's

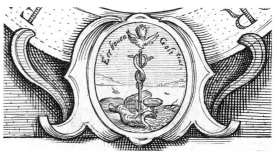

FIGURE 2
Jacob Matham (1571–1631)
Portrait of Hendrick Goltzius (after Hendrick Goltzius), 1618
Engraving, 21.7 x 13.2 cm
The Hearn Family Trust

Day of 1617. He left behind a tradition of printmaking carried forward by generations of Dutch artists together with a standard of artistic virtuosity matched only by history's greatest and most gifted figures.

Despite his artistic achievements and the centuries of praise that have only magnified them, Goltzius remains significantly lesser known than Dutch counterparts Rembrandt and Vermeer. Recent exhibitions have provided some remedy to the shortfall in name recognition. In 2003, The Metropolitan Museum of Art, New York; Rijksmuseum, Amsterdam; and the Toledo Museum of Art mounted the most expansive representation of the artist's work to date; *Hendrick Goltzius (1558–1617): Drawings, Prints and Paintings* included more than one hundred examples in these three media. Other large-scale projects have represented Goltzius as a major figure in Dutch art at the turn of the seventeenth century, perhaps the most significant of these being *Dawn of the Golden*

Age: Northern Netherlandish Art, 1580–1620, realized at the Rijksmuseum in 1993. Focused projects, such as *The "Pen-Works" of Hendrick Goltzius*, presented at the Philadelphia Museum of Art in 1992, introduced American audiences to the contributions Goltzius made to a distinct genre of art that blended the materials of drawing with the scale and canvas support of painting; *Goltzius and the Third Dimension*, held at the Clark Art Institute in Williamstown in 2001, explored Goltzius's intellectual response to the work of Dutch sculptor Willem Danielsz. Tetrode (c. 1525–1580). In 2005 the Davis Museum and Cultural Center at Wellesley College organized an exhibition featuring Goltzius's *Masterpieces* in the context of Mannerism titled *The "Master Prints" of Hendrick Goltzius and Mannerist Art*. Within California, the most recent exhibition dedicated to the works of Goltzius—particularly his prints—was mounted in 1992 by the Fisher Galleries at the University of Southern California. This exhibition, *Goltzius and the Classical Tradition*, emphasized Goltzius's interest in classical antiquity and his representations of mythological subjects. Now more than twenty years later, the current exhibition provides a complement to this previous project by examining two of Goltzius's most ambitious works as a printmaker—his series of engravings from the 1590s, the *Birth and Early Life of Christ* and the *Passion*—which are presented within the context of highlights of Goltzius's career in the graphic arts as well as examples of engraving by standard-setting predecessors Albrecht Dürer and Lucas van Leyden. It was in these devotional subjects, which effectively narrate the birth and death of Christ, that Goltzius chose to manifest the greatest performance of his exquisite skill as an engraver. During Goltzius's lifetime the *Birth and Early Life of Christ* (the *Masterpieces*) and the *Passion* brought him acclaim; in the decades after his death, the impact of these series reverberated through the words of famed Dutch poet and playwright Joost van den Vondel (1587–1679), whose poem "The Tombstone of Henrick Goltzius" of 1650 celebrated the skill and emotional appeal of these two career-defining series.

Both of these series reflect Goltzius's interest in emulating the art the past, at times to the point of deception. In Van Mander's biography of Goltzius, the *Masterpieces* are celebrated for their ability to fool collectors into believing that they were, in fact, acquiring examples of prints by Dürer or Lucas. In the dedication of the series, Goltzius addresses himself to his patron in Latin verses that identify Goltzius as a practitioner in the art of transformation. Indeed, in addition to his northern predecessors, Goltzius also emulated Italian artists in the six prints of this series. In the *Passion* series, Goltzius cited specific passages of engravings by both Dürer and Lucas, thereby establishing a permanent comparison of his treatment of this sacred subject to theirs. That Goltzius could use the technique of engraving to assimilate the graphic styles of German, Dutch, and Italian artists was a testament both to his knowledge and to his craft. As Van Mander summarized, "All these things mentioned together prove that Goltzius is a rare Proteus or Vertumnus in art, because he can transform himself to all forms of working methods."[2] For Goltzius's patrons, his deceptive performances served as references for an inner circle of sophisticated collectors.

The *Masterpieces* and *Passion* series also share dedications to figures of international reputation. In the case of the former, Goltzius dedicated his series to a member of the nobility, Duke Wilhelm V of Bavaria, a known collector and commissioner of art who awarded Goltzius a gold chain for the artistic brilliance he exhibited in the *Masterpieces*. The *Passion* series was dedicated to Cardinal-Archbishop Federico Borromeo, whose taste included a preference for northern landscape painting. Goltzius and Borromeo were both in Rome in the early 1590s, where Borromeo was developing his thoughts on the role of visual art in Catholic devotion, ideas he would eventually publish in the form of a treatise. In both cases, Goltzius attached his work to figures whose influence and status could help extend the reach of his ambition beyond his local audience of Haarlem or even the northern Netherlands.

It seems fitting, therefore, that this exhibition has been supported by dedicated patrons of the arts, Robert and Karen Hoehn, whose love of old master prints, drawings, paintings, and sculpture has led (among other things) to the creation of their impressive private collection as well as the establishment of a publicly accessible print study room and print galleries at the University of San Diego. Without their generosity and enthusiasm, this exhibition and the related publication would not have been possible. If Borromeo chided artists of the early seventeenth century for avoiding difficult things, despite their beauty, in favor of things that are undemanding,[3] then the Hoehns inspire fellow students of the visual arts to pursue life's truly difficult questions through a contemplation of beauty. As Goltzius was fortunate to find favor with the art-loving grandees of his day, we are likewise fortunate to have the support of these committed and enlightened patrons.

NOTES

[1] The most recent catalogue raisonné of prints by Goltzius was compiled by Marjolien Leesberg and published in the New Hollstein series; see F. W. H. Hollstein, *The New Hollstein: Dutch and Flemish Etchings, Engravings, and Woodcuts, 1450–1700* (Rotterdam: Sound and Vision Interactive; Amsterdam: Rijksprentenkabinet, Rijksmuseum, 2012).

[2] "Al dees verhaelde dinghen t'samen bewijsen/ Goltzium eene seldsame Proteus oft Vertumnus te wesen in de Const/ met hem in alle ghestalten van handelighen te connen herscheppen." Karel van Mander, *The Lives of the Illustrious Netherlandish and German Painters*, ed. and trans. Hessel Miedema (Doornspijk: Davaco), vol. 1, 398–99 (fol. 285r).

[3] "I have always noticed that we human beings have a natural defect: we avoid difficult things, no matter how beautiful they are, preferring instead things that are undemanding, no matter how unattractive they are." ["Semper ego animadverti esse hoc naturae nostrae vitium, ut ardua licet pulcherrima diffugiat, prona eadem ad pulchra minus, quippe quae facilia magis."] Federico Borromeo, *Sacred Painting; Museum*, ed. and trans. Kenneth S. Rothwell, Jr., introduction and notes by Pamela M. Jones (Cambridge, MA and London: The I Tatti Renaissance Library, Harvard University Press, 2010), 36–37.

11

FIGURE 1

Hendrick Goltzius (1558–1617)

The Annunciation (Birth and Early Life of Christ), 1594

Engraving, 47.9 x 35.5 cm

University of San Diego, Burgundian Fund, Acquired in Honor of Robert A. Hoehn

Goltzius's *Birth and Early Life of Christ*: Transformation and Renown

WILLIAM BREAZEALE

The *Birth and Early Life of Christ* series is in many ways about fame. By transforming his style six times, Hendrick Goltzius (1558–1617) performed a tour de force that dazzled his contemporaries, who must have asked the same questions that modern viewers do: Why and how did he "become" different artists? Why these subjects, why these artists? What did Goltzius gain?

The answers are many, and in many ways incomplete. But a closer look at the objects and the context in which they were created reveals much about Goltzius, about engraving, and about the artist's unique place in the Netherlands of the late sixteenth century. Part of this context is given by the dedication of the series, which appears in the *Annunciation* (fig. 1), the first event (but, as we shall see, not the first print) in the series. Isolated as if engraved on a vertical marble slab at the picture plane, it reads in translation:

> *Most serene prince and most illustrious master Wilhelm V,*
> *Count of the Rhenish Palatine and Duke of Bavaria, etc.:*
> *Just as Proteus among the waves transformed himself when he*
> *was prey to desire for the beautiful Pomona,*
> *Thus, O Prince, Goltzius, the admirable engraver and inventor,*
> *now transforms himself by means of a changeable art for you.*[1]

The dedicatory verse, the words being those of Goltzius's humanist friend Cornelius Schonaeus, compares him to the god Proteus, the son of Neptune who changed form to escape capture, and gives us one key to the meaning of the series.[2] The implication is that the art of engraving itself has the power to transform artists in the pursuit of fame.[3]

The visual experience of the *Birth and Early Life of Christ* series is enriched by reference to Karel Van Mander's (1548–1606) life of the artist. In addition to providing one of the most striking anecdotes in the artist's life, which as we shall see involved the *Circumcision*, the series provides the biography's overlying theme. Van Mander's friendship with the engraver meant that he knew the *Annunciation* and its inscription, so it is no wonder that he calls Goltzius a "Proteus or Vertumnus in art." Over and over again, disguise and transformation appear in the story of the artist's youth and maturity, but always linked to art and reputation. Engravings and biography offer many clues to a full reading, though both should be read with special attention.

Discussion of the *Birth and Early Life of Christ* series is complicated by issues of chronology. At least two orderings are possible, since Goltzius worked on the series of prints without reference to the sequence in which the episodes occur in the Bible. The *Visitation* and the *Holy Family with Infant St. John* date from 1593, others from 1594, and the order of execution within each year is difficult to know with any certainty. Most commentators begin with the

Circumcision and the *Adoration of the Magi*, since they are the two singled out for praise in Van Mander's biography. In these pages it seems best to look at the series as a whole, since the episodes, the stylistic models Goltzius used, and the context for which the series was made may well have been planned before the long process of engraving began.

The *Annunciation* (fig. 1) is a masterpiece of the engraver's art. The variety of burin lines is astonishing, from the graceful, swelling curves that cross and cross again to form the volumes of the archangel Gabriel's cloak and the clouds above him, to the tapered strokes of diminishing depth that end in the burst of light emanating from the dove of the Holy Spirit. The clear differentiation of textures, especially in the archangel's wings, is achieved with coarser or finer flicks of the burin as it travels across the plate to define volume. The iconography of this *Annunciation* is familiar to the Catholic world, with the Virgin interrupted at her reading by the lily-bearing Gabriel, her sewing basket lying on the floor nearby. A glory of angels reacts to the presence of the holy dove as it arrives. However, it is less clear which stylistic models Goltzius imitates—or is he imitating?

Other than the two prints in the series that are clearly in the manner of the engravers Albrecht Dürer and Lucas van Leyden, the series is generally agreed to be based on Italian models. Goltzius's trip to Italy in 1590–91 had transformed him through direct knowledge of the country and its art, so it is logical that such stylistic references should be present here. However, in the case of the *Annunciation*, specific correspondences to paintings or prints are especially difficult to pin down. Raphael's painting of the *Madonna del Cardellino* (1506) could provide the Virgin's head, Titian's *Annunciation* for the church of San Salvador in Venice (c. 1563–65) could provide the glory of angels,[4] but other artists favored in the search include the Umbrian Federico Barocci, the North Italian Correggio, and Federico Zuccaro, the latter known to Goltzius during his years in Rome.[5] Prints after these artists that Goltzius could have seen are many, but none of the correspondences is completely convincing.[6] Seen in a different light, however, this lack might be explained.

Visual sources provide one tool for looking at Goltzius's series, Van Mander's biographies and art theory another.[7] Goltzius's direct experience of Italian art may help to bring both into focus. Though by Van Mander's account the Rome of 1590–91 was a pestilent place with people dying in the streets, it was also an extremely active artistic community. The same Federico Zuccaro whom Goltzius met there was in 1593 to become the first *principe* of the city's Accademia di San Luca, the meeting place for artists and the model of many later academies across Europe. Still in its early days, the academy was where a certain artistic process was codified, though it had been in place informally for decades: the study of the best masters of the past with the object of creating one's own distinctive style.

Giovanni Battista Armenini's *De' veri precetti della pittura*, published in 1587, three years before Goltzius's Roman visit, even gives a list of ancient sculptures, frescoes, and paintings by Italian masters that are helpful to the young artist in training, with warnings against adopting too much of, for example, Michelangelo's style,[8] and mature artists like the Cavaliere d'Arpino would copy other masters perhaps as a stylistic 'refresher'.[9] The point is not that Goltzius would have followed Armenini's curriculum, though surviving drawings in his hand depict many of the same famous statues. Nor is it that Armenini's or even Van Mander's art theory would have necessarily served as a close guide, though this latter avenue has been explored fruitfully.[10] Rather, it is that the habitual incorporation and transformation of other artists' motifs and style in the search for one's own artistic vocabulary underlay the artistic process for Italian artists and, often, those who came to Rome from the North, for example in the case of Rubens, who arrived in Rome ten years after Goltzius. Goltzius's *Birth and Early Life of Christ* series could thus be seen as a series of artistic explorations of Italian and Northern styles, each one closely following a given master or region, with the enigmatic *Annunciation* representing Goltzius's own statement.

Goltzius's series differs from the one previously made for the same patron by Johannes Sadeler after Maerten de Vos in that it represents the Haarlem artist's own artistic thoughts rather than relying on preexisting designs by others. Let us look at the remaining objects in the series, then return to the *Annunciation*. In the *Visitation* (fig. 2), the influence of the northeastern Italian artist Parmigianino, known for the elongated grace of his figures, is clear, though a print after Federico Barocci by Gijsbert van Veen has been adduced as a model.[11] The two artists share the graceful draping seen here in the Virgin and Elizabeth, while the male figure in the background's elongated contrapposto pose seems more typical of the Parmese artist. The dog at lower right, interestingly, relates to those in Albrecht Dürer's woodcut *Passion* series.[12] Goltzius's burin work is characterized by long, deep strokes in the drapery, changing to hatched straight lines in the shadows and in the rational Renaissance architecture beyond. A basis in Parmigianino's figure types and architectural settings—coming more directly from his paintings than his prints—seems more convincing than a basis in Van Veen's print after Barocci of the same subject. There, the reversal of the figures, the figure types themselves, the setting in a stepped loggia, and the presence of foreground figures seem quite different. If so, an evocation of Parmigianino's serpentine grace would be appropriate for an artist seeking distinctive sixteenth-century styles.

The *Adoration of the Magi* (fig. 3) is a different matter. Its model is Lucas van Leyden's 1513 engraving of the same subject, adapted here from a horizontal to a vertical format. In each, the procession of figures winds into the background around a short dividing wall. Goltzius modifies the pose of the Virgin only slightly and moves Joseph behind her, while the distinctive beard of his kneeling king is similar to that of the standing king in Lucas's print. He uses sixteenth-century costumes, many with wild headdresses, with the young man standing behind the wall adapted from Lucas's *Portrait of a Young Man with*

Plena Deo virgo, cælesti Pneumate fœta,
Cognatam Helisaben montana per aspera visit;

Exultat sterilis fœcunda, exultat et infans
Iam tunc in grauidæ genitricis ventre Prophetes.

F.Estius.

FIGURE 2
Hendrick Goltzius (1558–1617)
The Visitation (Birth and Early Life of Christ), 1593
Engraving, 47.2 x 35.2 cm
Fine Arts Museums of San Francisco, Achenbach Foundation for Graphic Arts

E oi Reges Bethlen duce sydere ducti, *Deserto puerum in stabulo, et pia munera premunt*
Poplite submisso, peste Diademate, adorant. *Thuris rederat, Myrrheq, et divitis auri.*   F. X̃ffus.

FIGURE 3
Hendrick Goltzius (1558–1617)
Adoration of the Magi (Birth and Early Life of Christ), c. 1593
Engraving, 47.5 x 35.5 cm
Los Angeles County Museum of Art, Mary Stansbury Ruiz Bequest

a Skull of 1519.[13] Goltzius knew Lucas's prints in detail, for he imports the column's dog-headed decoration from Lucas's *Saint Jerome in his Study* of 1521.[14] His burin work is also adapted to Lucas's style, though his goal seems to have been effect rather than reproduction of technique: the light quality of Lucas's fine, even lines was achieved by using grey ink in some impressions.[15]

Was Goltzius's motivation for modeling the print after Lucas exclusively because of his admiration for his predecessor? Lucas's acclaim in the North was unquestioned, certainly. But along with Dürer he was collected assiduously by artists in Italy—the engraver Marcantonio Raimondi copied motifs from Lucas, Giulio Campagnola from Dürer—and Giorgio Vasari in his 1568 *Lives of the Artists* discussed both in detail in his life of Marcantonio. Other Italian art theorists, for example Giovan Paolo Lomazzo, regularly discussed the two Northerners as well.[16] In these works they were prized for their abilities in engraving, while Dürer was praised as the greater draughtsman. Seen in this light, the alternation in the *Birth and Early Life of Christ* series between Italian and Northern models begins to take on a different context. In the artistic world that Goltzius encountered in Italy, Dürer and Lucas were seen as the two most diligent and subtle technicians in the art of engraving, so that a printmaker could do no better than to combine their skills with Italian modes of picturing.

The pictorial developments of the Venetian Jacopo Bassano underlie the next engraving, the *Adoration of the Shepherds* (fig. 5), though a woodcut after Titian[17] provides the poses of Virgin and Child, also known in a painting by Titian now at Christ Church, Oxford, and an adaptation by Bassano himself now in the Royal Collection (fig. 4). Essentially a nocturne, a type brought to the fore by Bassano and popular among Venetian painters especially, it is lit from both natural and supernatural sources: the candle held by Joseph, the holy light of the Child himself, the glory of angels above, the lantern of the arriving shepherds, and the angelic light in the distant subsidiary scene of the Annunciation to the shepherds. Particularly the poses and figure type of the

FIGURE 4
Jacopo Bassano (c. 1510–1592)
Adoration of the Shepherds, c. 1546
Oil on canvas, 139.1 x 218.5 cm
The Royal Collection, acquired by Charles I

Cæli opifex, rerum dominus, Diuûm atâ hominum Rex   Et præsepe tenet, quem non capit arduus æther,
Nascitur en vilis tuguri sub paupere tecto,   Non mare, non tellus, non vasti machina mundi.

F. Estius.

FIGURE 5

Hendrick Goltzius (1558–1617)
Adoration of the Shepherds (Birth and Early Life of Christ), 1594
Engraving, 47.5 x 35.3 cm
Fine Arts Museums of San Francisco, California State Library Long Term Loan

Cernis vt octaua fit circuncisus Iesus
Luce puer, tenerè accipiensin coîpore vulnus,

Ad normam veteris legis, ritumq receptum,
Isacidis multos obseruatumq per annos.

C. Schonæus.

FIGURE 6
Hendrick Goltzius (1558–1617)
Circumcision (Birth and Early Life of Christ), 1594
Engraving, 47 x 35.6 cm
Los Angeles County Museum of Art, Anonymous Gift

peasant shepherds recall Bassano, likely known to the engraver through prints by the Sadeler brothers[18] and paintings he would have seen in Italy. Here the tour de force is the depiction of light and shadow, the close, dense burin work a development of that in the *Visitation*. The remarkable spatial recession of the cow's body and the fine detail of the background scene are further testimony of the artist's skill in handling.

Goltzius's *Circumcision* (fig. 6) is the most famous of Goltzius's engravings in the *Birth and Early Life of Christ* series. Reversing the composition of Dürer's woodcut of the same subject, it relies on the same central group of figures, while the candle-bearing figure at the foreground is seen from the back rather than the front.[19] Where Dürer's chapel is an anonymous barrel-vaulted space, Goltzius places the scene in the Brewer's Chapel in the Haarlem church of St. Bavo—and includes his self-portrait as the figure standing by the column. Goltzius rifles through Dürer's prints for other elements: the window at upper left has the same play of light as that in *St. Jerome in his Study* of 1514; Joseph is modeled on Dürer's *Apostle Simon* of 1523; the basin and ewer are present in *Pilate washing his hands* of 1512 from the *Small Passion*.[20] His representation of Dürer's technique is extremely close, the contrast between fine and deep lines especially successful in capturing effects of light as the eye travels over metal, fabric, stone, and glass.

In addition to its beauty and its virtuosic display, the *Circumcision* is celebrated as the object Goltzius used to dupe collectors, removing his monogram and aging it with smoke and creases and showing it in Rome, Venice, and Amsterdam as well as other places. Van Mander gives us the reaction:

> ...for when it was said or asked whether Goltzius could have made something like that, some people, who were not poor in art, replied that it was far beyond Goltzius to be able to make anything that good in the whole of his life; and that it was easily the best by Albert Dürer that had been seen. Some asserted further that Albert had engraved a particular plate which, when he died, he specified should remain hidden for a hundred years after his death and it could be printed only if his work was then still appreciated—and that this must be none other than that print.[21]

Within the context of Van Mander's biography of the engraver, with its continuing theme of brilliance, disguise, and deception, the anecdote has the ring of authenticity. A note of caution, however, is the fact that such anecdotes are part of a long tradition used to accent skill from ancient times: Pliny tells us that birds picked at the grapes in a wall painting by the Greek artist Zeuxis, for example. And the large size of Goltzius's print alone distinguishes it from Dürer's engravings in the eyes of modern viewers—it is over four inches taller and nearly as much wider than the *Saint Eustace* of c. 1501. Perhaps, though, truth does not matter in the end: both print and anecdote are part of the pursuit of fame.

The last print in the *Birth and Early Life of Christ* series, the *Holy Family with Infant St. John* (fig. 8), is based in Federico Barocci, the central Italian painter known best for his peaceful, tender compositions. Two engravings by Cornelis Cort after the Italian artist were available to Goltzius, one depicting the *Madonna of the Cat* of c. 1575 now in the National Gallery, London (fig. 7), the other depicting the *Madonna of the Bowl* of c. 1573 now in the Vatican, the latter of which places the Holy Family in an outdoor setting.[22] However, it is equally likely that Goltzius would have seen the *Madonna of the Cat* in person, as it was in Rome at the time of his visit.[23] It is by far the closer model. The engraver has taken over the pose of the Virgin almost literally, the exposed breast and proper right arm of the painting's figure being the only major differences. Other elements are transposed: the cat itself now traps a bird as it rears on a windowsill, a change paralleling the new position of Saint John the Baptist and Joseph. Again, except for the

distant landscape, the burin work is similar to that of the other Italian-based compositions with, in shaded areas, a slight moiré effect caused by the intersection of tapering curved lines. Interestingly, Goltzius here leaves the color of the paper as the bright white edge of fabrics, a technique he would later adopt from Lucas more directly in the *Adoration of the Magi*.

Federico Barocci is the last of the three Italian models chosen by Goltzius. The three, Parmigianino, Bassano, and Barocci, were praised for different qualities by the critic Raffaello Borghini, whose discussions of artists' distinctive points must have been current in Rome at the time of Goltzius's visit seven years after they were published.[24] Parmigianino was known for his figures' grace and life, sweet expressions, and beautiful landscapes.[25] Bassano painted with natural life and grace, especially animals and household items — here one thinks of details like the hat and water cask of the foreground figure in the *Adoration of the Shepherds*.[26] Barocci himself was prized for drawing, composition, and coloring that were marvels to see.[27] Leaving aside the landscapes of Parmigianino, then, the three artists are praised in terms that are all worthy of pursuit. Bassano and Barocci are praised for "colorito" as well, the one thing lacking in the medium of engraving. In addition to their role as tour de force and stylistic transformation, Goltzius's engravings in the manner of Lucas and

PRÆCVRSOR DOMINI LACTANTIS AB VBERE MATRIS QVEM PRÆCOGNOVIT SALIENS VTERO ABDITVS, HVNC ET
BLANDITVR PVERO PVER, ET COLLVDIT AMICE, INDICE MONSTRAVIT DIGITO CRESCENTIBVS ANNIS.

Dürer provide a demonstration of skill with the burin, the thing that makes it possible to mimic surfaces and textures visually without the use of color. This virtuosity, a "colorito" without color, may further explain the juxtaposition of Italian and Northern models within the series.

Let us return, finally, to the *Annunciation* and its role within the *Birth and Early Life of Christ* series. Could it have been part of Goltzius's enterprise to combine Parmigianino's sweet grace, Bassano's naturalness, and Barocci's drawing and sense of composition with the advanced technique taught him by Dürer's and Lucas's prints? One could point to elements within the *Annunciation* to support this view: the elongated beauty of the draped bodies, the light effects in the glory of angels, the triangle of gestures and glances, as well as the extremely fine textures. And, dating from 1594, it may have been the last print executed, as we have said. But these similarities remain stylistic and technical, rather than the more direct correspondences elsewhere in the series. The *Annunciation* represents something else again: if the end point of studying other artists is the development of one's own contribution to art, the difficulty of assigning specific predecessors to this print may be telling. Rather than performing the same function as the other prints in the series, it seems best suited to the role of a wider comment on Goltzius's experience of Italian art in the visual language of his recent Italian and Northern training. The wonder with which it, and the entire series, was received both by sixteenth-century aristocratic viewers—Wilhelm V awarded Goltzius a gold chain—and generations of print lovers has ensured its enduring fame and that of the artist as well.

NOTES

[1] "Serenissimo Principi, Ac Illustrissimo D[omi]no, D. Guilielmo.V. Comiti Palat. Rhe. Utriusq[ue] Bavariae Duci. Etc./ Ut medys Proteus se transformabat in undis,/ Formose cupido Pomone captus amore:/ Sic varia Princeps Tibi nunc se Goltzius arte/ Commutat, sculptor mirabilis, atq[ue] repertor." Translation my own, others in Huigen Leeflang, Ger Luijten, et al., *Hendrick Goltzius (1558–1617): Drawings, Prints and Paintings*, exh. cat. (Zwolle: Wanders Publishers, 2003), 210 and Walter Melion, "Piety and Pictorial Manner in Hendrick Goltzius's Early Birth and Early Life of Christ," in *Hendrick Goltzius and the Classical Tradition*, ed. Glenn Harcourt, exh. cat. (Los Angeles: Fisher Galleries, University of Southern California, 1992), 44.

[2] Vertumnus, the god of harvest and the suitor of Pomona, the goddess of abundance, had a similar faculty of transformation and was sometimes conflated with Proteus as here.

[3] For a fuller discussion of the Protean metaphor, see Walter Melion, "Karel Van Mander's 'Life of Goltzius': Defining the Paradigm of Protean Virtuosity in Haarlem around 1600," in *Cultural Differentiation and Cultural Identity in the Visual Arts*, ed. Susan Barnes and Walter Melion, *Studies in the History of Art 27*, Washington, 1989, 113–33, and Dorothy Limouze, "Engraving as Imitation: Goltzius and his Contemporaries," in *Nederlands Kunsthistorisch Jaarboek*, 42–43 (1991–92), 439–53.

[4] Melion, "Piety and Pictorial Manner," 50 for both.

[5] Barocci in Melion, "Piety and Pictorial Manner," 50 others Walter Strauss, *Hendrik Goltzius 1558–1617, the Complete Engravings and Woodcuts*, 2 vols. (New York: Abaris Books,1977) vol. 2, 584.

[6] According to the authors in *Hendrick Goltzius (1558–1617): Drawings, Prints and Paintings*, 214.

[7] *Hendrick Goltzius (1558–1617): Drawings, Prints and Paintings*; Melion, "Karel Van Mander's 'Life of Goltzius'" and Melion, "Piety and Pictorial Manner," respectively.

[8] Giovanni Battista Armenini, *De' veri precetti della pittura* (Ravenna and Bologna: 1587); for young artists and models to copy, see 61ff; for warnings against too much Michelangelo, see 63–64.

[9] For example in a drawing in the Crocker Art Museum, inv. no. 1871.329, discussed in Susan Anderson, Christine Giviskos, William Breazeale, and Christiane Andersson, *The Language of the Nude: Four Centuries of Drawing the Human Body*, exh. cat. (Sacramento and Aldershot, England: Crocker Art Museum and Ashgate, 2008), no. 5.

[10] As in Walter Melion's admirable articles: Melion, "Karel Van Mander's 'Life of Goltzius'" and Melion, "Piety and Pictorial Manner."

[11] Strauss, *Hendrik Goltzius 1558–1617, the Complete Engravings and Woodcuts*, 576; Melion, "Piety and Pictorial Manner," 50 for Parmigianino; *Hendrick Goltzius (1558–1617): Drawings, Prints and Paintings*, 215 for Van Veen after Barocci.

[12] As pointed out in *Hendrick Goltzius (1558–1617): Drawings, Prints and Paintings*, 215. The prints in question are more specifically Bartsch 8, *Christ at the Column*, with the dog facing the viewer; Bartsch 10, *Christ Carrying the Cross*, with the dog rearing and facing the background.

[13] David Acton, "The Northern Masters in Goltzius's Meisterstiche," in *Bulletin of the Museums of Art and Archaeology, University of Michigan* 4 (1981), 44.

[14] Idem.

[15] *Hendrick Goltzius (1558–1617): Drawings, Prints and Paintings*, 214. Grey ink was used from the earliest times in etchings, see Gregory Jecmen, "Color printing and tonal etching, innovative techniques in the Imperial city, 1487–1536," in Gregory Jecmen and Freyda Spira, *Imperial Augsburg: Renaissance Prints and Drawings 1475–1540*, exh. cat. (Washington, D.C. and Farnham, Surry: National Gallery of Art in association with Lund Humpries, 2012), 67–101.

[16] See Bart Cornelis and Jan Piet Filedt Kok, "The Taste for Lucas van Leyden prints," in *Simiolus: Netherlands Quarterly for the History of Art*, 26, no. 1/2 (1998) 18–20, 27–33.

[17] *Hendrick Goltzius (1558–1617): Drawings, Prints and Paintings*, 214.

[18] Idem.

[19] And perhaps also related to the figure in the Pilate scene of the *Small Passion*, Melion, "Piety and Pictorial Manner," 47.

[20] *Hendrick Goltzius (1558–1617): Drawings, Prints and Paintings*, 212-13 and notes give history of these identifications; Acton, "The Northern Masters in Goltzius's Meisterstiche," 47 for basin and ewer.

[21] " … want doe geseyt/ oft ghvraeght was/ of Goltzius sulcx wel mocht hebben ghedaen/ werdt gheantwoort van eenighe/ die niet slecht zijn in de Const/ dat het wijt daer van was/ dat Goltzius zijn leven soo goet en soude connen doen: jae was wel t'beste dat sy van Albert Durer hadden gesien. Eenige voeghden noch daer hy/ dat Albert had ghesneden een besonder plaet/ die hy in zijn overlijden bevel verborghen te houden een hondert Jaren nae zijn doot: en indien dan zijn dinghen noch in achtinge waren/ datmense drucke soude/ en anders niet/ en dit most enckel dese Print wese." Karel van Mander, *The Lives of the Illustrious Netherlandish and German Painters*, ed. and trans. Hessel Miedema (Doornspijk: Davaco, 1994–99), vol. 1, 397, (fol. 284v).

[22] *Hendrick Goltzius (1558–1617): Drawings, Prints and Paintings*, 214.

[23] Strauss, *Hendrik Goltzius 1558–1617, the Complete Engravings and Woodcuts,* 574.

[24] *Il Riposo*, Florence, 1584.

[25] Ibid., 442.

[26] Ibid., 563.

[27] Ibid., 568.

FIGURE 1
Hendrick Goltzius (1558–1617)
Christ Carrying the Cross (The Passion), 1596–98
Engraving (actual size)
University of San Diego
Purchased with Funds from Robert and Karen Hoehn

26

Silent Oratory in Goltzius's *Passion*

VICTORIA SANCHO LOBIS

*I*n the final years of the sixteenth century, Hendrick Goltzius (1558 – 1617) set out to create a series of twelve engravings representing the Passion of Christ. At this stage in his career, he was a well-established and widely celebrated printmaker in control of his own printing press. Despite the existence of a few mysteriously incomplete compositions — among them, the much-celebrated *Adoration of the Shepherds* (illustrated on page 47) — Goltzius's *Passion* series served as his last fully realized statement as an engraver.[1] Not monumental in scale, the prints are nevertheless invested with profound ambition, reflected in their execution and also in the dedication of the series to the art collector and theologian Cardinal-Archbishop Federico Borromeo. Each of the plates was thoroughly worked, leaving only a few passages of reserve to create striking descriptions of natural, artificial, and heavenly light. Elaborately described architectural and natural environments provide the settings for Goltzius's *Passion* — whether geometrically composed rooflines or craggy outcroppings of rock. Compressed within a few square inches of space, each composition also includes many more figures than the Gospel accounts required. In some cases, such as *Christ Carrying the Cross* (fig. 1), there are more figures than could possibly be counted. To emphasize the density of the crowd surrounding Christ, Goltzius describes one of his captors as a fragment of a figure represented at the far right margin only by a right foot, a few fingers of a right hand, and the tip of a sword. Indeed, in these details and throughout the series one discovers intriguing compositional choices executed with delicate and nuanced engraved lines, so subtly employed that the labor of the artist's hand dissolves into the successful illusion of volume and depth, gesture and expression.

Biographers and scholars have long recognized the popularity of Goltzius's *Passion* and its importance for the artists of successive generations.[2] But the series as a whole has not captured the imagination of these writers to the same extent that his *Masterpieces* series has done so thoroughly from the time of its creation up through the present day.[3] Recent exhibition catalogues and scholarly essays have emphasized Goltzius's motivation for producing his *Passion* series as a means of demonstrating his ability to match the staggering technical achievements of Lucas van Leyden (c. 1494–1533) and Albrecht Dürer (1471–1528), twin forces in the art of engraving not only in the Netherlands and German principalities, but throughout Western Europe.[4] One cannot deny that Goltzius actively sought out this type of comparison — through explicit citation of these artists, through the dedication of his most ambitious prints to aristocrats and theologians of international position, and through

the very application of his finely wrought craft. In his *Passion* series, Goltzius brought to bear the full range of his graphic vocabulary: dense cross-hatching, varied spacing for parallel hatching, selective stippling, the use of swelling and tapering lines to suggest volume, and the dramatic use of the blank paper to render the effects of light. Yet in his 1604 biography of Goltzius, friend and fellow Haarlem-based artist Karel van Mander (1548–1606) summarized the *Passion* series as "very pleasing, totally in the manner of Lucas van Leyden, although in posing the figures and in other details he applied a particular manner which is no less to be esteemed, nor worse."[5] For an artist such as Goltzius, about whom lengthy poems of praise were written even during his lifetime, the judgment "no less to be esteemed, nor worse" hardly constitutes a generous assessment of quality. A few decades later, poet and political operative Constantijn Huygens (1596–1687) echoed Van Mander's words and cemented a now centuries-long tradition of interpreting Goltzius's *Passion* through the lens of its artistic antecedents.[6] Though Goltzius courted this comparison to his illustrious predecessors, it has also blinded viewers to the original contributions that he made to the visual tradition of representing the Passion. This essay seeks to recognize in Goltzius's *Passion* his attempt not only to demonstrate skill and virtue, but also to negotiate the challenging intellectual and theological climate of the late sixteenth century. In the aftermath of iconoclasm and the suppression of Catholic ritual in the northern Netherlands and during the emergence

FIGURE 4
Hendrick Goltzius (1558–1617)
Christ Crowned with Thorns (The Passion), 1597
Engraving (actual size)
University of San Diego
Purchased with Funds from Robert and Karen Hoehn

FIGURE 5
Lucas van Leyden (c. 1494–1533)
The Large Ecce Homo, 1510
Engraving, 28.7 x 45.2 cm
The British Museum, London

of post-Reformation doctrine governing the use of images for Christian devotion, Goltzius chose for his final statement as an engraver the challenging subject of Christ's Passion. As we will see, Goltzius addressed his series to multiple audiences simultaneously, effectively exploiting the inherent flexibility of the print medium while also demonstrating the expressive potential of the art of engraving.[7]

Goltzius's debt to Dürer and Lucas must be acknowledged (figs. 2–4). There is no question that their repeated treatments of the Passion and the widespread acclaim for these prints set a standard that Goltzius sought to reach. As has been observed, figure types and compositional conceits are drawn from the examples these great printmakers left behind. But the citations are usually not as explicit as they are in the *Masterpieces* series. Unlike Dürer's *Engraved Passion*, which features close, even claustrophobic interior settings, Goltzius often choses elaborate outdoor spaces defined by a seemingly endless pattern of receding building façades. Indeed, Goltzius's description of architecture distinguishes his series from those of Dürer and Lucas. Though Lucas chose an elaborate architectural setting for his *Ecce Homo* of 1510 (fig. 5), which was issued as a single subject, his *Passion* series prints and many of his devotional subjects are characterized more by natural rather than by built landscapes.[8] Likely inspired by buildings seen during Goltzius's Italian voyage of the early 1590s, the porticos and rooflines found in his series provide the viewer with an elaborate if perhaps superfluous setting, one that distracts from the central action as much as it provokes the viewer to decipher the location for each scene. Even in his choice of format—vertically oriented rectangular compositions of modest but not minute scale—Goltzius set his series apart from the

FIGURE 6

Hendrick Goltzius (1558–1617)

The Last Supper (The Passion), 1598

Engraving (actual size)

University of San Diego

Purchased with Funds from Robert and Karen Hoehn

31

small engraved *Passions* of Lucas and Dürer (1521 and c. 1510, respectively) and the larger scale woodcut *Passion* of Dürer and circular engraved *Passion* of Lucas (c. 1500 and 1509). At a total count of twelve subjects, Goltzius again chose a middle ground—fewer subjects than the sixteen of Dürer's *Engraved Passion* and the fourteen of Lucas's small *Passion* series and more than Lucas's nine subjects of the *Circular Passion*.[9]

In his *Last Supper* (fig. 6), Goltzius divides the composition into nearly equal halves. The lower half serves as the place for the essential narrative content, and the upper half provides elaboration for that narrative setting beyond all descriptions found in the Gospel texts. Luke provides the most detailed description of the setting. In his account, a man bearing a pitcher of water leads the disciples to a house in which there is a guest chamber, "a large upper room furnished." [Luke 22: 11–12] Goltzius sets his *Last Supper* in what appears to be a lower courtyard placed between two buildings rather than contained within one. In his division of the compositional space, and indeed in his imaginative and elaborate description of the setting, Goltzius expresses the multiple functions for his *Passion*: to represent what was perhaps the most sacred of narratives in keeping with the demands of his local Protestant audience; to

FIGURE 7
Pieter Saenredam (1597–1665)
Interior of the Grote Kerk at Haarlem, 1636–37
Oil on oak, 59.5 x 81.7 cm
National Gallery, London, Salting Bequest, 1910

recognize the emerging stipulations for devotional art expressed by the reforming figures within the Catholic church; and to appeal to the prevailing taste among international art collectors for a self-conscious performance of technique, an ability to cite the art of the past while matching it stroke for stroke and line for line.

While Dürer and Lucas created their *Passion* prints in the early moments of the Reformation of the Catholic church, Goltzius engaged these subjects in a much more contentious climate with specific regard to the status of devotional images.[10] Debates about whether devotional images were to be understood as inherently idolatrous had been waged since the earliest days of Christianity, with allowances for images made on the grounds that they could help instruct the illiterate to whom sacred texts were not accessible. The sixteenth century ushered in a renewed demand for the removal of devotional images and all forms of adornment within churches.

When Goltzius was still learning his craft, widespread iconoclasm erupted in 1566 in Antwerp and elsewhere in the northern and southern Netherlands, involving the removal and destruction of altarpieces, rood screens, tabernacles, stained glass, and prayer books. In May of 1578, Goltzius's adopted city of Haarlem witnessed its own form of iconoclasm: a day-long attack on devotional objects within the Catholic cathedral of St. Bavo, later to be renamed the Great Church by the Dutch Reformers who occupied it.[11] What could not be eradicated through removal or destruction could be erased from sight through whitewashing, as early seventeenth-century paintings of the interior depict (fig. 7). Paintings of saints and biblical narratives were replaced with white walls and paintings of sacred texts, such as the Ten Commandments and a Gospel account of the Last Supper. Having arrived in Haarlem in 1577, Goltzius witnessed this dramatic transformation of the city's grandest church firsthand. During these transitional years, Goltzius also worked closely with Antwerp-based print publisher Philips Galle, a relationship that brought Goltzius into contact with the Jesuits and with Counter-Reformation projects based in Antwerp such as the Polyglot Bible.[12] The resolutions of the Council of Trent, whose final session concluded in 1563, set forth summary guidelines for the use and production of devotional imagery. But the question was far from settled, and prescriptions for the use of images in Christian worship continued to proliferate, with pamphlets and treatises published in the Netherlands and elsewhere throughout the later decades of the sixteenth century and early decades of the seventeenth.[13]

One of these treatises was authored by Cardinal-Archbishop Federico Borromeo of Milan, the dedicatee of Goltzius's *Passion* series. In naming Borromeo in the *Last Supper*, the de facto frontispiece to the series, Goltzius placed his *Passion* in a context broader than the decidedly Protestant milieu of Haarlem and the northern Netherlands, where the celebration of Roman Catholic mass and the administration of the sacraments could not be performed in public after 1580. Goltzius had also received a print privilege in April of 1595 from Habsburg Emperor Rudolf II that was valid for six years; this early form of copyright also required Goltzius to eschew subjects that conflicted with the Catholic faith or the laws of the Holy Roman Empire.[14] But while engaging Passion iconography and the discussions about its place in Christian devotion, Goltzius's extensive and explicit citation of Dürer and Lucas also gave his prints a firm foundation within a northern European visual tradition. The very selection of the Passion as the subject for his final statement as an engraver affirmed Goltzius's position in the pantheon of northern European artists such as Martin Schongauer (c. 1448–1491) and his own teacher Dirck Volkertsz. Coornhert (1522–1590), who completed a series of the *Life and Passion of Christ* after Maarten van Heemskerck in 1548.[15] At the time of Goltzius's dedication, Borromeo was still in Rome, where he began assembling his art collection, now the heart of the Ambrosiana collection in Milan. Borromeo had a particular preference for northern art. His collection included paintings by Flemish landscape specialists Paul Bril and Jan Brueghel the Elder, who became a regular correspondent and life-long friend. In 1596, the earliest year attached to Goltzius's *Passion*, Borromeo received a letter from Jan Brueghel promising him several prints of "happy and devout subjects." A folio still in the Ambrosiana may correspond to this promised shipment; it includes biblical subjects by Hans Aldegrever and a nearly complete set of Dürer's *Engraved Passion*.[16] Given Borromeo's interest in northern art and Goltzius's choice to dedicate his *Passion* series to the Cardinal-Archbishop, it is worth considering the extent to which Goltzius's representation of the Passion subjects corresponded to Borromeo's beliefs about the potentially devotional and didactic function of images.

In his *De Pictura Sacra (Sacred Painting)*, Borromeo concerns himself with the proper depiction of devotional subjects as well as the placement of paintings in sacred buildings. He emphasizes the general desire for naturalism on the one hand and for historical accuracy on the other. He draws on ancient and Patristic texts to support his ideas, thereby suggesting the legitimacy of visual representations in a devotional context through its long-standing tradition. *Sacred Painting* was first published in 1624, but the ideas it conveys were most likely developed while Borromeo studied in Rome, between 1586 and 1601. It was during this time in Rome that Borromeo and Goltzius would have crossed paths. Goltzius traveled to Italy in 1590–91 and included Rome as the centerpiece of his itinerary.

In one of the most distinctive chapters of *Sacred Painting*, Borromeo likens the role of the painter to that of the orator: "Just as an orator performs his duty best if he speaks with the passion and energy needed to move people's minds, so too is it the great charge of painting … to implant in the mind feelings of reverence, fear, and sadness whenever demanded by the subject."[17] Curiously, in Goltzius's *Passion* series, the emotional appeal to the viewer often seems indirect. Goltzius's Christ—at times impassive and motionless—does not inspire profound empathy. His face registers little emotion. In anatomical terms, he is often the least well defined within a given composition. Goltzius also consistently places his viewer at a distance from the narrative action. In every print in the series, one if not several figures occupy the foreground space and consequently the viewer's attention. Nowhere is this choice clearer than in the *Resurrection* (fig. 8). The ascending Christ is placed in the upper third of the composition, and the dramatic burst of light—described by the abundant use of the reserve—sets off the figure of the attendant angel rather than the Christ figure. In this final subject of the series Goltzius elides several moments from the Gospel accounts, adapting the narrative provided by Matthew in greatest detail. Goltzius describes Mary Magdalene and at least two other figures approaching the sepulchre, where an angel is seated on top of the stone at the sepulchre's entrance; "[the angel's] countenance was like lightning, and his raiment white as snow" as Matthew writes [Matthew 28:3]. But closer to the viewer Goltzius places the guards, some of whom have collapsed or seem to be asleep, others of whom shrink in fear from the brilliant spectacle. Closest still to the viewer is a guard who turns away from the narrative action altogether. His head, adorned with feathery plumes, reaches at least to half the total length of the field of the image. As is seen in several other scenes from the series, this figure is dressed in an elaborate costume adorned with fancy trimmings—puffs with slits at the shoulder, elbow, and knee; shin-high boots; and a complex mechanism for adorning and attaching the codpiece. It is this guard figure whose costume is clearly the closest to contemporary fashion. His position and posture further emphasize that it is he who is closest to the viewer in spatial and in metaphorical terms. Borromeo wrote of the Resurrection: "the truth is that the watchmen were completely unaware that the Savior had come out of the tomb and it was only later, after the angel rolled aside the stone, that they were woken up by the noise and were terrified."[18] Goltzius goes a step beyond Borromeo in providing a watchman who remains oblivious even after the stone has been rolled away and the angel had appeared.

In his *Resurrection* and elsewhere in the series, Goltzius offers a Passion narrative in which the figure of Christ is not presented as an object of devotion. In the *Crucifixion* (fig. 10), for example, the crucified Christ is set in the middle ground of the composition, again with a group of fancifully adorned figures in the foreground space. While Goltzius conforms to Borromeo's later insistence on the representation of Christ crucified with the two thieves—that is, with the thieves also shown as crucified and not strung up or otherwise affixed to crosses—he does not offer this scene of Crucifixion as one that should inspire meditative devotion. Goltzius was certainly capable of this type of rendering, as is clear from a number of paintings produced in the early years of the seventeenth century, such as the *Man of Sorrows with Chalice* of 1614 (fig. 9), in which the body of Christ is presented in proximity to the picture plane.[19] In an earlier engraving of 1585 (fig. 11), Goltzius also represents the Crucifixion with more direct appeal to the viewer in terms of an identification with the figure

FIGURE 8
Hendrick Goltzius (1558–1617)
The Resurrection (The Passion), 1596
Engraving (actual size)
University of San Diego
Purchased with Funds from Robert and Karen Hoehn

of Christ. Again, in his *Passion*, Goltzius presents a Crucifixion that challenges the viewer to identify his or her role in the narrative; the figure of Christ is not offered as a stimulus for personal identification. In this subject and throughout the series, Goltzius chooses to create a *Passion* that emphasizes narrative and setting over empathic representations of Christ (fig. 12). It should not surprise us, then, that in the four copy drawings that Peter Paul Rubens made very shortly after the publication of Goltzius's *Passion*, not one of them includes the figure of Christ. They are rather studies of the supporting figures in the narrative, curious to Rubens because of their position, expressions, and garments.[20] It is also worth remarking that Goltzius's *Passion* includes no Man of Sorrows and no Deposition, a subject connected with the problematic Deposition rite, which was increasingly removed from devotional practice by the end of the sixteenth century.[21] In short, Goltzius actively restricts his viewers from engaging in meditative contemplation of the body of Christ, or, in other words, the perception of the pictured body of Christ as an icon. Rather, viewers of his *Passion* are engaged with a more literary experience of the elements of the Passion narrative and, further, with the complex and engaging description of the figures that participate in and observe the events of the Christ's Passion.

Unlike many other examples from his printed oeuvre—indeed the *Masterpieces* series, for example—Goltzius's *Passion* does not include inscriptions. The images do not support or engage a supplied text; rather, they act as a substitute for text. So while Goltzius refrains from presenting Christ as an *imago pietatis* in the strictest sense, he also presents his images as independent from scripture. In fact Goltzius's series occupies a middle ground in terms of the print market in the post-Reformation Netherlandish context—between the

FIGURE 9
Hendrick Goltzius (1558–1617)
Man of Sorrow with a Chalice, 1614
Oil on panel, 89 x 78.7 cm
Princeton University Art Museum

FIGURE 10
Hendrick Goltzius (1558–1617)
The Crucifixion or Calvary (The Passion), 1596–98
Engraving (actual size)
University of San Diego
Purchased with Funds from Robert and Karen Hoehn

38

Dum morior rigidi sublatus in arbore trunci,
Vulneribus sano vulnera vestra meis.

FIGURE 11
Hendrick Goltzius (1558–1617)
The Crucifixion, 1585
Engraving (actual size)
Collection of Robert and Karen Hoehn

penchant for Old Testament subjects and illustrated Bibles that were popular in the Dutch Reformed communities of the northern Netherlands and the explicitly meditative and emotionally engaging prints popular among Catholics in the southern Netherlands.[22] Borromeo's comparison of the painter to the orator suggests a way in which Goltzius sought to emphasize the story of the Passion without investing his representation of it with the implied presence of divinity. While his Christ cannot intercede on behalf of his viewer, the narrative elements and their elaborate description incite the viewer to consider his or her place in relation to these events. At times deplorable for their actions and vicious expressions, the secondary narrative figures such as Pilate, Caiaphas, and Christ's unnamed tormentors are not models for pious behavior but rather mirrors for introspection. Finally, the application of his technical virtuosity to this most sacred narrative also refers Goltzius's viewer to the work of God as enacted by man.[23] In all these ways, Goltzius was able to appeal to multiple audiences—those who would see his prints as works of art independent of their devotional subjects; those who continued to believe in the power of images to inspire piety; and those whose foremost dedication to sacred texts could be supported by the parallel representation of biblical narratives in visual form, especially as realized by small-scale engravings suitable for private, if not individual, engagement.

During Goltzius's lifetime and immediately thereafter the market for his *Passion* series was vibrant, even voracious. The plates he engraved went through four editions, the edition Goltzius published himself and editions published after his death by three different Dutch print publishers—Dancker Danckerts, Clement de Jonghe, and Frederick de Wit. In addition to the publication of these editions of the plates actually engraved by Goltzius, at least seven different sets of copies of the series were produced before the end of the seventeenth century, some in more than three different editions. In other words, within one hundred years of their production, Goltzius's set of twelve engraved plates had inspired the creation of seven additional sets of plates, which were themselves printed in multiple versions. We can therefore imagine that thousands, if not tens of thousands, of impressions of this series circulated within Europe.[24]

By the year 1600, Hendrick Goltzius had retired his printmaking tools to turn his full attention to the art of painting. He was forty-two years old and would live for another seventeen years. He made this choice despite decades of international acclaim and the independence of his own printing press, which he established in 1582. Over the intervening centuries the interest in his prints demonstrates that Goltzius had indeed achieved enough in the art of printmaking to hold his place in the pantheon of graphic artists. His *Passion* series not only testifies to this achievement, it also reflects his remarkable ability to embed within a series of silent and static images the dynamic potential to communicate ideas directed at several different audiences. Through its layers of narrative detail, virtuoso technical performance, and devotional inspiration, Goltzius's *Passion* continues to charge the viewers of today with a call to individual interpretation.

NOTES

I would like to thank Robert Hoehn, Jessica Keating, Seth Lobis, Stephanie Schrader, and Anne Woollett for discussing this essay with me at various stages of its development.

[1] On the *Adoration of the Shepherds* as Goltzius's last engraving see Huigen Leeflang, "De laatste gravure van Hendrick Goltzius?," *Kunstlicht* 11 (1990), nos. 2/3, 33–40. The most current catalogue of prints by Goltzius was assembled by Marjolein Leesberg and published in the New Hollstein series; see F. W. H. Hollstein, *The New Hollstein: Dutch and Flemish Etchings, Engravings, and Woodcuts, 1450–1700* (Rotterdam: Sound and Vision Interactive; Amsterdam: Rijksprentenkabinet, Rijksmuseum, 2012).

[2] Huigen Leeflang, Ger Luijten, et al., *Hendrick Goltzius (1558–1617): Drawings, Prints and Paintings*, exh. cat. (Zwolle: Wanders Publishers, 2003), cat. no. 80, 223–25.

[3] See especially Walter Melion, "Hendrick Goltzius's Project of Reproductive Engraving," *Art History* 13, no. 4 (December, 1990), 458–87. For additional bibliographic references see William Breazeale's essay in this publication.

[4] Larry Silver, "Imitation and Emulation: Goltzius as Evolutionary Reproductive Engraver," in Timothy Riggs and Larry Silver, *Graven Images: The Rise of Professional Printmakers in Antwerp and Haarlem, 1540-1640*, exh. cat. (Evanston, IL: Northwestern University Press, 1993), 83–84; see also Bart Cornelis and Jan Piet Filedt Kok, "The Taste for Lucas van Leyden Prints," *Simiolus* 26, nos. 1/2 (1998), 37–39.

[5] "Nae dese dinghen heeft hy in't Jaer 1597 van hem late uytgae een heel Passie/ die wonder vehaeghlijck is/ en gantsch op de manier van Lucas van Leyde/ gebruykende doch in de stellinghen der beelden en anders een seker wijse/ die niet verachtlijcker oft argher en is." Karel van Mander, *The Lives of the Illustrious Netherlandish and German Painters*, ed. and trans. Hessel Miedema (Doornspijk: Davaco, 1994–99), vol. 1, 398–99 (fol. 285r).

[6] "Wie dit wonderbare genie langs de kortste weg wil doorgronden, moet zijn De Geboorte des Heren en Het Lijden des Heren bekijken, getuigenissen van de grootste durf. Wat kenmerkend is voor Albrecht Dürer, Lucas van Leyden en …, genieën die hun weerga niet kennen, heeft hij in die werken zo knap tot uitdrukking gebracht, dat men zou denken dat deze kunstenaars in hem weer op de wereld zijn teruggekeerd." Constantijn Huygens, *Mijn jeugd*, trans. and ed. C. L. Heesakkers (Amsterdam: Em. Querido's Uitgeverij B.V., 1987), 78.

[7] James Bloom has pursued this line of interpretation in the context of another print by Goltzius. See James J. Bloom, "Mastering the Medium: Reference and Audience in Goltzius's Print of the Circumcision," *Nederlands Kunsthistorisch Jaarboek* 52 (2001), 79–103. For a more general discussion in the same volume on multiplicity of possible interpretations for sixteenth-century printed images see Jan Van der Stock, "Ambiguous Intentions, Multiple Interpretations: An 'Other' Look at Printed Images from the Sixteenth Century," *Nederlands Kunsthistorisch Jaarboek* 52 (2001), 19–29.

[8] As discussed by Ilja Veldman in *Lucas van Leyden en de Renaissance*, exh. cat. (Ludion: Antwerp, 2001), 49–50.

[9] Dürer's *Engraved Passion* includes a Man of Sorrows as its first subject and Peter and Paul Healing a Lame Man as the final subject. Despite its aberration from Passion iconography, the latter has been included in the *Engraved Passion* series because of its dimensions and date of execution. See Rainer Schoch, Matthias Mende, and Anna Scherbaum, *Albrecht Dürer: Das druckgraphische Werk*, 3 vols. (Munich, London, New York: Prestel, 2001) vol. 1, 125–52.

[10] On this subject see David Freedberg, *Iconoclasm and Painting in the Revolt of the Netherlands, 1566–1609* (London: Garland, 1988).

[11] On the fate of St. Bavo after the iconoclasm, see Mia M. Mochizuki, *The Netherlandish Image after Iconoclasm, 1566–1672: Material Religion in the Dutch Golden Age* (Aldershot, England and Burlington, VT: Ashgate Publishing, 2008).

[12] See Manfred Sellink, "Een teruggevonden *Laatste Oordeel* van Hendrick Goltzius: Goltzius' relatie met de Antwerpse uitgever Philips Galle," *Nederlands Kunsthistorisch Jaarboek* 41–42 (1991–92), 145–58. For further discussion of Goltzius's appeal to Catholic viewers, see Walter Melion, "*Oratio* and *Reformatio* in Hendrick Goltzius's *Adoration of the Magi* of 1605," in Walter Melion, *The Meditative Art: Studies in the Northern Devotional Print, 1550–1625*, Early Modern Catholicism and the Visual Arts Series, Vol. 1 (Philadelphia: Saint Joseph's University Press, 2009), 295–329.

[13] For a description of the tracts on the proper use of images that circulated in the Netherlands, see Freedberg, *Iconoclasm and Painting in the Revolt of the Netherlands, 1566–1609*. A more recent account and analysis of these texts can be found in Koenraad Jonckheere, *Antwerp Art after Iconoclasm: Experiments in Decorum, 1566–1585* (Brussels: Mercatorfonds, 2012), 31–42.

[14] The terms of the privilege also required Goltzius to send three impressions of each published print to Rudolf II. For the complete stipulations of the privilege see Lawrence W. Nichols, "Hendrick Goltzius—Documents and Printed Literature Concerning His Life," *Nederlands Kunsthistorisch Jaarboek* 41–42 (1991–92), 91. See also Nadine Orenstein, Huigen Leeflang, Ger Luijten, and Christiaan Schuckman, "Print Publishers in the Netherlands, 1580–1620," in *Dawn of the Golden Age: Northern Netherlandish Art, 1580–1620*, Ger Luijten and Ariane van Suchtelen, eds. exh. cat. (Amsterdam and Zwolle: Rijksmuseum and Waanders Uitgevers, 1993), 181.

[15] For further discussion of Coornhert, his philosophy, and its expression in the field of printmaking, see Ilja M. Veldman, *De Wereld tussen Goed en Kwaad: Late Prenten van Coornhert*, exh. cat., Stedelijk Museum het Catharina Gasthuis (The Hague: SDU Uitgeverij, 1990).

[16] Pamela M. Jones, *Federico Borromeo and the Ambrosiana: Art Patronage and Reform in Seventeenth-Century Milan* (Cambridge: Cambridge University Press, 1993), 272–77. See elsewhere in this publication for a discussion of Borromeo's prescriptions about the devotional, didactic, and documentary role of the visual arts.

[17] "Ac sicuti ad Oratoris munus plurimi refert, ea, quae dicuntur, enunciari cum affectu et vigore, qui movere animos possit, ita magnum picturae opus erit, … ut inserant animo pios sensus metumque et dolorem quotiescumque res postulabit." Federico Borromeo, *Sacred Painting; Museum*, ed. and trans. Kenneth S. Rothwell, Jr., introduction and notes by Pamela M. Jones (Cambridge, MA and London: The I Tatti Renaissance Library, Harvard University Press, 2010), 47.

[18] "Prodiit enim ex tumulo Salvator, ita ut vigiles illi nihil sentirent. Postea interiecto aliquo temporis spacio, cum Angelus monumenti lapidem evolveret, excitati strepitum sensere, territique fuerent." Borromeo, *Sacred Painting*, 89.

[19] Goltzius represented Christ as a figure inspiring pity on several occasions; see Lawrence W. Nichols, *The Paintings of Hendrick Goltzius, 1558–1617: A Monograph and Catalogue Raisonné* (Doornspijk: Davaco, 2013), cat. nos. A-14, A-15, A-16, A-17, and A-20.

[20] Kristin Belkin, *Rubens, Copies and Adaptations from Renaissance and Later Artists: German and Netherlandish Artists*, Corpus Rubenianum Ludwig Burchard XXVI, part I, 2 vols. (London: Harvey Miller, 2009), nos. 72, 108–10. For further discussion of the artistic exchange between Goltzius and Rubens, see Filip Vermeylen and Karolien De Clippel, "Rubens and Goltzius in Dialogue: Artistic Exchanges between Antwerp and Haarlem During the Revolt," *De Zeventiende Eeuw* 28, no. 2 (2012), 138–60.

[21] As discussed in Amy Powell, *Depositions: Scenes from the Late Medieval Church and the Modern Museum* (New York: Zone Books, 2012).

[22] For further discussion of the use of prints in daily life, including the religious context, see Jan van der Waals, *Prenten in de Gouden Eeuw: Van Kunst tot Kastpapier*, exh. cat. (Rotterdam: Museum Boijmans van Beuningen, 2006), 80–103. See also Ilja Veldman, "Convictions and Polemics: Protestant Imagery in the Sixteenth Century," in Ilja Veldman, *Images for the Eye and Soul: Function and Meaning in Netherlandish Prints, 1450–1650* (Leiden: Primavera Pers, 2006), 91–117, and James Clifton and Walter S. Melion, eds. *Scripture for the Eyes: Biblical Illustration in Netherlandish Prints of the Sixteenth Century*, exh. cat. (New York: Museum of Biblical Art, 2009).

[23] On the performance of *teyckenconst* as a means of expressing and inspiring devotion, see Walter S. Melion, "Self-Imaging and the Engraver's *Virtu*: Hendrick Goltzius's *Pietà* of 1598," *Nederlands Kunsthistorisch Jaarboek* 46 (1995), 105–43.

[24] The production of these many editions and sets of copies was no doubt aided by the survival of all of Goltzius's preparatory drawings for the series as well as the complete set of copper plates—all of which are extant even today. See Marjolein Leesberg's entries for the *Passion* series as well as her discussion of the deceptive copies produced possibly by members of the Goltzius workshop in the Introduction to *The New Hollstein Goltzius* volumes as cited above. I wish to thank Marjolein Leesberg for her insights on the relative popularity of Goltzius's *Passion* series and its production after the artist's death.

SUGGESTED FURTHER READING

Bialler, Nancy. *Chiaroscuro Woodcuts: Hendrick Goltzius (1558–1617) and His Time*. Exh. cat. Amsterdam and Ghent: Rijksmuseum and Snoeck-Ducaju & Zoon, 1992.

Clifton, James. *A Portrait of the Artist, 1525–1825: Prints from the Collection of the Sarah Campbell Blaffer Foundation*. Exh. cat. Houston: Museum of Fine Arts, Houston, 2005.

Clifton, James and Walter S. Melion. *Scripture for the Eyes: Bible Illustration in Netherlandish Prints of the Sixteenth Century*. Exh. cat. New York and London: Museum of Biblical Art in association with D Giles Limited, 2009.

Falkenburg, Reindert, Jan Piet Filedt Kok, and Huigen Leeflang. *Goltzius-Studies: Hendrick Goltzius (1558–1617)*. *Nederlands Kunsthistorisch Jaarboek 1991–92*. Volume 42–43. Zwolle: Waanders Uitgevers, 1993.

Goddard Stephen H. and James A. Ganz. *Goltzius and the Third Dimension*. Exh. cat. Williamstown, MA: Sterling and Francine Clark Art Institute, 2001.

Harcourt, Glenn, ed. *Hendrick Goltzius and the Classical Tradition*. Exh. cat. Los Angeles: Fisher Gallery, University of Southern California, 1992.

Hoehn, Robert. *The Gospel According to Rembrandt*. Exh. cat. San Diego: University of San Diego, 2004.

Leeflang, Huigen, Ger Luijten, et. al. *Hendrick Goltzius (1558–1617): Drawing, Prints and Paintings*. Exh. cat. Zwolle: Waanders Publishers, 2003.

Luijten, Ger and Ariane van Suchtelen, eds. *Dawn of the Golden Age: Northern Netherlandish Art, 1580–1620*. Exh. cat. Amsterdam and Zwolle: Rijksmuseum and Waanders Uitgevers, 1993.

Melion, Walter S. *The Meditative Art: Studies in the Northern Devotional Print, 1550–1625*. Early Modern Catholicism and the Visual Arts Series, Vol. 1. Philadelphia: Saint Joseph's University Press, 2009.

Nichols, Lawrence W. *The "Pen Works" of Hendrick Goltzius. Philadelphia Museum of Art Bulletin*. Volume 88, Number 373/374. Philadelphia: Philadelphia Museum of Art, 1992.

Peters, Emily J. *The Brilliant Line: Following the Early Modern Engraver, 1480–1650*. Exh. cat. Providence: Museum of Art, Rhode Island School of Design, 2009.

Riggs, Timothy and Larry Silver. *Graven Images: The Rise of Professional Printmakers in Antwerp and Haarlem, 1540–1640*. Exh. cat. Evanston, IL: Mary and Leigh Block Gallery, Northwestern University, 1993.

EXHIBITION CHECKLIST

Checklist is organized alphabetically by
artist name and then chronologically.
Height precedes width in the dimensions.
If no state designation is indicated, there is
only one state known.

JOHANNES PIETERSZ. BEERENDRECHT
(active 1614–45), publisher

Anonymous (after Hendrick Goltzius
and Jacob Matham)
Portrait of Hendrick Goltzius, 1617
Engraving, 20.6 x 17.9 cm
(sheet and platemark)
[New Hollstein 241 (Matham), copy a;
New Hollstein 750 (Goltzius), copy a]
The Hearn Family Trust

ALBRECHT DÜRER (1471–1528)

Madonna on the Grassy Bank, 1503
Engraving, 11.8 x 14.1 cm
(trimmed within platemark)
[Meder 31; Schoch 36]
Los Angeles County Museum of Art
Graphic Arts Council Fund
M.66.13

The Lamentation (Engraved Passion), 1507
Engraving, 12 x 7.6 cm (sheet and platemark)
[Meder 14; Schoch 56]
Los Angeles County Museum of Art
Graphic Arts Council Fund
M.70.68.12

Agony in the Garden (Engraved Passion), 1508
Engraving, 12 x 7.6 cm (sheet and platemark)
[Meder 4; Schoch 46]
Los Angeles County Museum of Art
Graphic Arts Council Fund
M.70.68.2

The Betrayal of Christ (Engraved Passion), 1508
Engraving, 12 x 7.6 cm (sheet and platemark)
[Meder 5; Schoch 47]
Los Angeles County Museum of Art
Graphic Arts Council Fund
M.70.68.3

Man of Sorrows (Engraved Passion), 1509
Engraving, 12 x 7.6 cm (sheet and platemark)
[Meder 3; Schoch 45]
Los Angeles County Museum of Art
Graphic Arts Council Fund
M.70.68.1

The Crucifixion (Engraved Passion), 1511
Engraving, 12 x 7.6 cm (sheet and platemark)
[Meder 13; Schoch 55]
Los Angeles County Museum of Art
Graphic Arts Council Fund
M.70.68.11

The Circumcision (Life of the Virgin), 1511
Woodcut, 29.2 x 21 cm (image and sheet)
[Meder 198; Schoch 176]
Los Angeles County Museum of Art
Gift of Herman and Ruth Engel in honor
of the museum's 40th anniversary, the
40th anniversary of the Graphic Arts Council,
and Herman Engel's 100th year
M.2007.215.2

*Christ Before Caiaphas
(Engraved Passion)*, 1512
Engraving, 12 x 7.6 cm (sheet and platemark)
[Meder 6; Schoch 48]
Los Angeles County Museum of Art
Graphic Arts Council Fund
M.70.68.4

Christ Before Pilate (Engraved Passion), 1512
Engraving, 12 x 7.6 cm (sheet and platemark)
[Meder 7; Schoch 49]
Los Angeles County Museum of Art
Graphic Arts Council Fund
M.70.68.5

The Flagellation (Engraved Passion), 1512
Engraving, 12 x 7.6 cm (sheet and platemark)
[Meder 8; Schoch 50]
Los Angeles County Museum of Art
Graphic Arts Council Fund
M.70.68.6

*Christ Crowned with Thorns
(Engraved Passion)*, 1512
Engraving, 12 x 7.6 cm (sheet and platemark)
[Meder 9; Schoch 51]
Los Angeles County Museum of Art
Graphic Arts Council Fund
M.70.68.7
Reproduced on page 28

Ecce Homo (Engraved Passion), 1512
Engraving, 12 x 7.6 cm (sheet and platemark)
[Meder 10; Schoch 52]
Los Angeles County Museum of Art
Graphic Arts Council Fund
M.70.68.8

*Pilate Washing His Hands
(Engraved Passion)*, 1512
Engraving, 12 x 7.6 cm (sheet and platemark)
[Meder 11; Schoch 53]
Los Angeles County Museum of Art
Graphic Arts Council Fund
M.70.68.9

*The Carrying of the Cross
(Engraved Passion)*, 1512
Engraving, 12 x 7.6 cm (sheet and platemark)
[Meder 12; Schoch 54]
Los Angeles County Museum of Art
Graphic Arts Council Fund
M.70.68.10

The Entombment (Engraved Passion), 1512
Engraving, 12 x 7.6 cm (sheet and platemark)
[Meder 15; Schoch 57]
Los Angeles County Museum of Art
Graphic Arts Council Fund
M.70.68.13

*Christ's Descent into Hell
(Engraved Passion)*, 1512
Engraving, 12 x 7.6 cm (sheet and platemark)
[Meder 16; Schoch 58]
Los Angeles County Museum of Art
Graphic Arts Council Fund
M.70.68.14

The Resurrection (Engraved Passion), 1512
Engraving, 12 x 7.6 cm (sheet and platemark)
[Meder 17; Schoch 59]
Los Angeles County Museum of Art
Graphic Arts Council Fund
M.70.68.15

*Peter and Paul Healing a Lame Man
(Engraved Passion)*, 1513
Engraving, 12 x 7.6 cm (sheet and platemark)
[Meder 18; Schoch 60]
Los Angeles County Museum of Art
Graphic Arts Council Fund
M.70.68.16

HENDRICK GOLTZIUS (1558–1617)

The Crucifixion, 1585
Engraving, 21.3 x 15.7 cm (trimmed to plate-
mark with thread margins at lower edge)
[Strauss 221; New Hollstein 30 ii/ii]
Collection of Robert and Karen Hoehn
Reproduced on page 39

The Body of Christ Supported by Angels
(after Bartholomeus Spranger), 1587
Engraving, 34.8 x 25.4 cm (sheet and platemark)
[Strauss 254; New Hollstein 339]
Crocker Art Museum, Gift of Alan Templeton
2012.127

Hercules and Cacus, 1588
Chiaroscuro woodcut, line block in black
and tone blocks in tan and olive green,
40.7 x 32.4 cm (sheet trimmed to borderline);
signature in dark tone block is faint
[Strauss 403 ii/iv; Bialler 25 i/vi color variant C;
New Hollstein 304 i/iii, color variant E]
Leitman-Butler Collection

The Great Hercules or 'Knollenman', 1589
Engraving, 57 x 40.7 cm (platemark);
58.7 x 42.4 cm (sheet)
[Strauss 283 i/ii; New Hollstein 156 i/ii]
Leitman-Butler Collection

The Holy Family under the Cherry Tree, 1589
Engraving, 24.4 x 19.9 cm
(sheet and platemark)
[Strauss 264; New Hollstein 32 i/ii]
Crocker Art Museum, Gift of Alan Templeton
2012.105

Holy Family
(after Bartholomeus Spranger), c. 1589
Engraving, 28.3 x 21.2 cm
(trimmed within platemark)
[Strauss 281; New Hollstein 338]
Getscher-Wilkinson Collection, Cleveland

Judith with the Head of Holofernes, early 1590s
Pen and dark brown ink, brush and grey
wash and blue and white opaque watercolor,
partially darkened, on brown laid paper,
20.3 x 16.6 cm
[Reznicek 20; Breazeale et. al. 17]
Crocker Art Museum, E. B. Crocker Collection
1871.142

Portrait of Dirck Volkertsz. Coornhert, 1591
Engraving, 47.6 x 34.9 cm (image)
[Strauss 287 iii/iii without frame;
New Hollstein 211 iii/iii without frame]
Fine Arts Museums of San Francisco
Achenbach Foundation for Graphic Arts
Endowment Fund
1965.68.177

Portrait of Dirck Volkertsz. Coornhert, 1591
Engraving, 52.2 x 41.4 cm
(sheet and platemark)
[Strauss 287 iii/iii with frame;
New Hollstein 211 iii/iii with frame]
Collection UCLA Grunwald Center for the
Graphic Arts, Hammer Museum
1970.12.1

Pygmalion and Galatea, 1593
Engraving, 32.4 x 21.8 cm
(trimmed within platemark)
[Strauss 315 iv/iv; New Hollstein 157 iv/iv]
Los Angeles County Museum of Art
Gift of Ernest Raboff Gallery
60.67.6

Portrait of Hans Bol, 1593
Engraving, 26 x 18 cm (platemark);
26.7 x 18.7 cm (sheet)
[Strauss 316; New Hollstein 209 i/ii]
Los Angeles County Museum of Art
Mary Stansbury Ruiz Bequest
M.88.91.288

The Visitation
(Birth and Early Life of Christ), 1593
Engraving, 47.2 x 35.2 cm (image)
[Strauss 318 iii/v; New Hollstein 9 ii/ii]
Fine Arts Museums of San Francisco
Achenbach Foundation for Graphic Arts
1963.30.12449
Reproduced on page 16

Holy Family with Infant St. John
(Birth and Early Life of Christ), 1593
Engraving, 47.3 x 35.6 cm
(sheet and platemark)
[Strauss 317 iii/v; New Hollstein 13 iii/iii]
Los Angeles County Museum of Art
Mary Stansbury Ruiz Bequest
M.88.91.109
Reproduced on page 23

Adoration of the Magi
(Birth and Early Life of Christ), c. 1593
Engraving, 47.5 x 35.5 cm
(platemark); 48.3 x 36.5 (sheet)
[Strauss 320 ii/v; New Hollstein 12 i/ii]
Los Angeles County Museum of Art
Mary Stansbury Ruiz Bequest
M.88.91.538
Reproduced on page 17

The Circumcision
(Birth and Early Life of Christ), 1594
Engraving, 47 x 35.6 cm (sheet and platemark)
[Strauss 322 iii/v; New Hollstein 11 ii/ii]
Los Angeles County Museum of Art
Anonymous Gift
M.84.232.2
Reproduced on page 20

The Circumcision
(Birth and Early Life of Christ), 1594
Engraving, 47.8 x 35.3 cm
(trimmed within platemark)
[Strauss 322 iii/v; New Hollstein 11 ii/ii]
Fine Arts Museums of San Francisco, California
State Library Long Term Loan
A015760

Adoration of the Shepherds
(Birth and Early Life of Christ), 1594
Engraving, 47.2 x 35 cm (image)
[Strauss 319 iii/v; New Hollstein 10 ii/ii]
Fine Arts Museums of San Francisco, California
State Library Long Term Loan
L509.1966
Reproduced on page 19

The Annunciation
(Birth and Early Life of Christ), 1594
Engraving, 47.9 x 35.5 cm (platemark);
49.4 x 36.9 cm (sheet)
[Strauss 321 ii/iv; New Hollstein 8 i/vi]
University of San Diego, Burgundian Fund
Acquired in Honor of Robert A. Hoehn
PC2013.3
Reproduced on page 12

Christ Before Pilate (The Passion), 1596
Engraving, 20.4 x 13.5 cm (platemark);
21 x 14.4 cm (sheet)
[Strauss 332 i/ii; New Hollstein 21]
University of San Diego, Purchased with Funds
from Robert and Karen Hoehn
PC2010.2.5

The Entombment (The Passion), 1596
Engraving, 20.2 x 13.5 cm
(sheet and platemark)
[Strauss 334 i/ii; New Hollstein 27]
University of San Diego, Purchased with
Funds from Robert and Karen Hoehn
PC2010.2.11

The Resurrection (The Passion), 1596
Engraving, 20.3 x 13.5 cm
(sheet and platemark)
[Strauss 333 i/ii; New Hollstein 28]
University of San Diego, Purchased with
Funds from Robert and Karen Hoehn
PC2010.2.12
Reproduced on page 36

Pietà, 1596
Engraving, 17.7 x 12.7 (sheet and platemark)
[Strauss 331 ii/ii; New Hollstein 31 ii/ii]
Collection of Robert and Karen Hoehn

The Agony in the Garden (The Passion), 1597
Engraving, 20.3 x 13.6 cm (platemark);
21 x 14.1 cm (sheet)
[Strauss 342 i/ii; New Hollstein 18]
University of San Diego, Purchased with
Funds from Robert and Karen Hoehn
PC2010.2.2

Christ Before Caiaphas (The Passion), 1597
Engraving, 20.3 x 13.5 cm (sheet and platemark)
[Strauss 343 i/ii; New Hollstein 20]
University of San Diego, Purchased with
Funds from Robert and Karen Hoehn
PC2010.2.4

The Flagellation (The Passion), 1597
Engraving, 20.4 x 13.5 cm (platemark);
21.1 x 14.2 cm (sheet)
[Strauss 339 i/ii; New Hollstein 22]
University of San Diego, Purchased with
Funds from Robert and Karen Hoehn
PC2010.2.6
Reproduced on page 41

Christ Crowned with Thorns (The Passion), 1597
Engraving, 20.2 x 13.4 cm (platemark);
21 x 14.3 cm (sheet)
[Strauss 340 i/ii; New Hollstein 23]
University of San Diego, Purchased with
Funds from Robert and Karen Hoehn
PC2010.2.7
Reproduced on page 29

Ecce Homo (The Passion), 1597
Engraving, 20.4 x 13.6 cm (platemark);
20.9 x 14.2 cm (sheet)
[Strauss 341 i/ii; New Hollstein 24]
University of San Diego, Purchased with
Funds from Robert and Karen Hoehn
PC2010.2.8

The Last Supper (The Passion), 1598
Engraving, 20.1 x 13.4 cm
(sheet and platemark)
[Strauss 356 i/ii; New Hollstein 17 i/iii]
University of San Diego, Purchased with
Funds from Robert and Karen Hoehn
PC2010.2.1
Reproduced on page 31

The Betrayal of Christ (The Passion), 1598
Engraving, 20.4 x 13.5 cm (platemark);
20.9 x 14.3 cm (sheet)
[Strauss 355 i/ii; New Hollstein 19 ii/ii]
University of San Diego, Purchased with
Funds from Robert and Karen Hoehn
PC2010.2.3

Christ Carrying the Cross (The Passion), 1596–98
Engraving, 20.3 x 13.7 cm (platemark);
20.9 x 14.3 cm (sheet)
[Strauss 353 i/ii; New Hollstein 25]
University of San Diego, Purchased with
Funds from Robert and Karen Hoehn
PC2010.2.9
Reproduced on page 26

The Crucifixion or Calvary
(The Passion), 1596–98
Engraving, 20.1 x 13.4 cm
(sheet and platemark)
[Strauss 354 i/ii; New Hollstein 26]
University of San Diego, Purchased with
Funds from Robert and Karen Hoehn
PC2010.2.10
Reproduced on page 38

Adoration of the Shepherds, 1598–1600
Engraving, 18.4 x 14.8 cm
(trimmed within platemark)
[Strauss 362 i/v; New Hollstein 14 i/vi]
Collection of Robert and Karen Hoehn
Reproduced on page 47

Self-Portrait, c. 1605
Black chalk, colored chalk, and white opaque
watercolor on parchment, 9.8 cm diameter
[Reznicek supplement, K257a]
The Hearn Family Trust
Reproduced on page 11

The Artist's Emblem, 1609
Pen and brown ink, 15 x 8.9 cm
[Reznicek 197]
Crocker Art Museum
E. B. Crocker Collection, 1871.143
Reproduced on page 7

LUCAS VAN LEYDEN (c. 1494–1533)

The Raising of Lazarus, c. 1507
Engraving, 28.3 x 20.3 cm
(sheet and borderline)
[New Hollstein 42]
Los Angeles County Museum of Art
Gift of Joseph B. Koepfli
M.61.22

Susanna and the Two Elders, c. 1508
Engraving, 15.2 x 20.3 cm
(sheet and platemark)
[New Hollstein 33]
Collection UCLA Grunwald Center
for the Graphic Arts, Hammer Museum
Purchased with funds provided by the
Friends of the Graphic Arts
2006.31.1

The Return of the Prodigal Son, c. 1510
Engraving, 18.2 x 24.8 cm
(sheet and platemark)
[New Hollstein 78 i/iii]
Fine Arts Museums of San Francisco
Achenbach Foundation for Graphic Arts
Gift of Michael G. Berolzheimer
in memory of Michael Berolzheimer
1998.201.26

Christ Crowned with Thorns
(The Passion), 1521
Engraving, 11 x 7.5 cm (image)
[New Hollstein 49 i/iii]
Fine Arts Museums of San Francisco
Achenbach Foundation for Graphic Arts
1963.30.572
Reproduced on page 28

The Entombment (The Passion), 1521
Engraving, 11.5 x 7.4 cm (sheet and platemark)
[New Hollstein 54 ii/iii]
Fine Arts Museums of San Francisco
Achenbach Foundation for Graphic Arts
1963.30.569

JACOB MATHAM (1571–1631)

Portrait of Hendrick Goltzius
(after Hendrick Goltzius), 1617
Engraving, 43.3 x 28.8 cm
(trimmed to platemark)
[New Hollstein 241 ii/ii (Matham);
New Hollstein 750 ii/ii (Goltzius)]
The Hearn Family Trust
Reproduced on page 4

Portrait of Hendrick Goltzius
(after Hendrick Goltzius), 1618
Engraving, 21.7 x 13.2 cm (platemark);
21.9 x 13.6 cm (sheet)
[New Hollstein 242 i/v (Matham);
New Hollstein 751 i/vi (Goltzius)]
The Hearn Family Trust
Reproduced on page 8

Portrait of Hendrick Goltzius
(after Hendrick Goltzius), published in 1620
Engraving, 21.4 x 12.8 cm
(trimmed within platemark)
[New Hollstein 242 ii/v (Matham);
New Hollstein 751 ii/vi (Goltzius)]
The Hearn Family Trust

Portrait of Hendrick Goltzius
(after Hendrick Goltzius), published in 1630
Engraving, 21.7 x 13.1 cm (platemark);
24 x 15.5 cm (sheet)
[New Hollstein 242 iv/v (Matham);
New Hollstein 751 v/vi (Goltzius)]
The Hearn Family Trust

MARCANTONIO RAIMONDI
(c. 1480–before 1534)

Circumcision of Christ (Life of the Virgin)
(after Albrecht Dürer), c. 1510–30
Engraving, 29 x 21.2 cm (image)
[Bartsch XIV.406.632]
Fine Arts Museums of San Francisco
Achenbach Foundation for Graphic Arts
1963.30.36355

Abbreviations:

Bartsch: Bartsch, Adam von. *The Illustrated Bartsch*. Walter L. Strauss, ed. New York: Abaris Books, 1978–.

Bialler: Bialler, Nancy. *Chiaroscuro Woodcuts: Hendrick Goltzius (1558–1617) and His Time.* Exh. cat. Amsterdam and Ghent: Rijksmuseum and Snoeck-Ducaju & Zoon, 1992.

Breazeale, et. al.: Breazeale, William with Cara Denison, Stacey Sell, and Freyda Spira. *A Pioneering Collection: Master Drawings from the Crocker Art Museum*. Sacramento and London: Crocker Art Museum and Paul Holberton Publishing, 2010.

Meder: Meder, Joseph. *Dürer-Katalog: Kupferstiche/Radierungen/Holzschnitte.* Vienna: Verlag Gilhofer & Ranschburg, 1932.

New Hollstein (Hendrick Goltzius): Hollstein, F. W. H., *The New Hollstein: Dutch and Flemish Etchings, Engravings, and Woodcuts, 1450–1700.* Marjolein Leesberg, compiler. Huigen Leeflang, editor. Rotterdam: Sound and Vision Interactive; Amsterdam: Rijksprentenkabinet, Rijksmuseum, 2012.

New Hollstein (Lucas van Leyden): Hollstein, F. W. H., *The New Hollstein: Dutch and Flemish Etchings, Engravings, and Woodcuts, 1450–1700.* Jan Piet Filedt Kok, compiler. Ger Luitjen, editor. Rotterdam: Sound and Vision Interactive; Amsterdam: Rijksprentenkabinet, Rijksmuseum, 1996.

New Hollstein (Jacob Matham): Hollstein, F. W. H., *The New Hollstein: Dutch and Flemish Etchings, Engravings, and Woodcuts, 1450–1700.* Léna Widerkehr, compiler. Huigen Leeflang, editor. Rotterdam: Sound and Vision Interactive; Amsterdam: Rijksprentenkabinet, Rijksmuseum, 2007.

Reznicek: Reznicek, E. K. J., *Die Zeichnungen von Hendrick Goltzius*. 2 vols. Utrecht: Haentjens Dekker & Gumbert, 1961.

Reznicek, supplement: Reznicek, E. K. J., "Drawings by Hendrick Goltzius, Thirty Years Later, Supplement to the 1961 Catalogue Raisonné," *Master Drawings*, vol. XXXI, no. 3 (Fall 1993) 215–278.

Schoch: Schoch, Rainer, Matthias Mende, and Anna Scherbaum. *Albrecht Dürer: Das druckgraphische Werk*. 3 vols. Munich, London, New York: Prestel, 2001.

Strauss: Strauss, Walter L. *Hendrik Goltzius, 1558–1617: The Complete Engravings and Woodcuts*. 2 vols. New York: Abaris Books, 1977.

Cum privil. Sa. Cæ. Mtis.
HGoltzius Fecit
I. Matham excud.

Hendrick Goltzius (1558–1617)
Adoration of the Shepherds, 1598–1600
Engraving (actual size)
Collection of Robert and Karen Hoehn